£5.9

Chilterns

Compiled by
Terry Marsh

publishing

Mapping sourced from Ordnance Survey®

Text: Terry Marsh
Photography: Terry Marsh
Editors: Geoffrey Sutton
Crawford Gillan
Designer: Doug Whitworth

© Jarrold Publishing 2002

 This product includes mapping data licensed from Ordnance Survey ® with the permission of the Controller of Her Majesty's Stationery Office. © Crown Copyright 2002. All rights reserved. Licence number 100017593. Pathfinder is a registered trade mark of Ordnance Survey, the national mapping agency of Great Britain.

Jarrold Publishing ISBN 0-7117-2087-8

While every care has been taken to ensure the accuracy of the route directions, the publishers cannot accept responsibility for errors or omissions, or for changes in details given. The countryside is not static: hedges and fences can be removed, field boundaries can alter, footpaths can be rerouted and changes in ownership can result in the closure or diversion of some concessionary paths. Also, paths that are easy and pleasant for walking in fine conditions may become slippery, muddy and difficult in wet weather, while stepping-stones across rivers and streams may become impassable.

If you find an inaccuracy in either the text or maps, please write or e-mail Jarrold Publishing at one of the addresses below.

First published 2002
by Jarrold Publishing

Printed in Belgium
by Proost NV, Turnhout. 1/02

Jarrold Publishing
Pathfinder Guides, Whitefriars,
Norwich NR3 1TR
E-mail: pathfinder@jarrold.com
www.jarroldpublishing.co.uk/
pathfinders

Front cover: The Grand Union Canal
Previous page: Stokenchurch

Contents

Keymap

SCALE 1:312 500 or 1 INCH to 5 MILES *1CM to 3.1 KM*

0   2   4   6   8   10 KILOMETRES   15

0   2   4   6   MILES 8   10

KEYMAP HEIGHTS SHOWN IN FEET

Introduction

The routes and information in this book have been devised specifically with families and children in mind. All the walks include points of interest as well as a question to provide an objective.

If you, or your children, have not walked before, choose from the shorter walks for your first outings, although none of the walks is especially demanding. The purpose is not simply to get from A to B, but to enjoy an exploration, which may be just a steady stroll in the countryside.

The walks are graded by length and difficulty, but few landscapes are truly flat, especially those among the Chilterns. Even short walks may involve some ascent, but this is nowhere excessive. Details are given under Route Features in the first information box for each route. The precise nature of the ground underfoot, however, will depend on recent weather conditions. If you do set out on a walk and discover the going is harder than you expected, or the weather has deteriorated, do not be afraid to turn back. The route will always be there another day, when you are fitter or the children are more experienced or the weather is better.

Bear in mind that the countryside also changes. Landmarks may disappear, gates may becomes stiles, rights-of-way may be altered. Among the Chiltern beechwoods, it is especially important to realise that in autumn many of the paths are obliterated by fallen leaves, and this means having to pay close attention to waymarking or, in the absence of waymarking, the general direction followed by the path.

In Hodgemoor Wood

With the aid of this book and its maps you should be able to enjoy many interesting family walks in the Chilterns.

Marlow Bridge and the Thames Path

The Chilterns

Exactly what comprises 'The Chilterns' is a matter of conjecture. Certainly it includes the Chilterns Area of Outstanding Natural Beauty (AONB) along with the Chiltern Hundreds, though the two do not have the same boundary. Whatever the extent of the Chilterns, their main focus is the Chiltern Hills, an undulating collection of low hills extending from the Thames in the south-west to Ivinghoe Beacon in the north-east.

The Chilterns were designated an Area of Outstanding Natural Beauty in 1965, and cover 322 sq miles (833 sq km), and with a boundary of 276 miles (444km). They spread across the counties of Oxfordshire (30%), Buckinghamshire (51%) and Bedfordshire (8%).

The Chiltern Hundreds is a collection of now obsolete local government units. Traditionally, a 'hundred' is part of the English local government system, thought originally to be the equivalent in size to 100 'hides', a hide being the amount of land needed to support one peasant family. So, in a sense, a hundred was a loose community of 100 families. The expression first appeared during the reign of Edmund I (939–946), but there is evidence to show that, by then, it was already a well-established concept. The Chiltern Hundreds comprise five hundreds in Oxfordshire and three in Buckinghamshire.

The natural beauty of the Chilterns has long been popular with politicians, poets and writers. Chequers, not far from Ellesborough, is the official country residence of the Prime Minister, and Dorney Wood the official residence of the Chancellor of the Exchequer. Prime Minister Benjamin Disraeli lived at Hughenden Manor and is buried in the graveyard there; poet Thomas Gray lived around Stoke Poges and is also buried there (although his name does not appear on the family vault). Clement Attlee lived near Great Missenden and W.H. Smith, founder of the high-street bookshop chain, lies buried at Hambleden.

The Chilterns scenery is a mixture of chalk grassland, scrub, woodland, farm fields, holloways (sunken lanes), streams and hedgerows that collectively provide habitats for hundreds of different plants and animals. A single square metre of chalk turf may contain between thirty and forty separate plant species. In the sunshine, butterflies are everywhere and in the woods badgers are common, while foxes and weasels hunt field mice in the grass.

Birds of prey are part of the diversity of the Chilterns nature, too. They have lived in a natural balance with their prey for thousands of years. It is only man who upsets this, as he did when the red kite was exterminated, save for a stronghold in central Wales, at the end of the 19th century. Since then, birds have been reintroduced from Spain, and red kites are again a common feature above the fields and woodlands of the Chilterns. Buzzards are here, too, but they are fewer in number.

Millfield Wood, Hughenden

Above all, the great delight of the Chilterns must be their extensive beech woodlands, to some extent man-managed to provide wood for the furniture-making industries that grew up around High Wycombe and Chesham. In autumn, especially, the woodlands are a great

Almshouses in Mapledurham

delight, bathed in golden light made more intense by the hues of beech leaves. At this time, wandering in the woodlands requires an alertness not needed to the same extent at other times of the year. The paths are deeply padded with fallen leaves that rustle musically beneath one's feet, but which obscure the way through the woods. Thankfully, most of the routes are waymarked by white arrows painted on trees, leaving the walker free to concentrate on the array of flora and fauna and the simple pleasure of mature woodlands.

The closeness of the Chilterns to London has made this an immensely popular weekend retreat as well as an important link in the nation's trading network. Across the Chilterns runs the Ridgeway Path, encountered quite a few times in these walks, and the Icknield Way, both of which make good use of the chalk ridges and form part of a prehistoric trade route across the southern part of England.

In spite of the proximity to England's capital, few of the walks found in this book are overused, and walkers, away from the honeypots along the Thames, are only infrequently encountered. The opportunity to wander peacefully, enjoy the sound of silence (usually disrupted only by a foraging squirrel or scuttling pheasant) and to escape the brouhaha and stresses of modern life is a treasure to be kept and a delight to be savoured.

1 *Hodgemoor Wood*

START Chalfont St Giles
DISTANCE 1½ miles (2.4km)
TIME 1 hour
PARKING Car park along Botterells Lane
ROUTE FEATURES Woodland paths and trails

Hodgemoor Wood lies to the west of Chalfont St Giles and is a Site of Special Scientific Interest (SSSI) with diverse wildlife habitats. This short walk follows a waymarked route – the Coppice Trail – through the wood.

Leave the car park, having located the tall signpost for 'The Coppice Trail', which sets off through lovely stands of silver birch and beech.

The trail is waymarked throughout by yellow-banded poles. The first

> **Hodgemoor Wood** is named after the Saxon word *Hodd* for the folk of this area. This ancient wood remains one of the largest areas of semi-natural woodland in Buckinghamshire and extends to 292 acres (118 ha). It was designated a Site of Special Scientific Interest in 1991.

In Hodgemoor Wood

PUBLIC TRANSPORT Buses to Chalfont St Giles
REFRESHMENTS Pub on A355 and in Chalfont St Giles
PUBLIC TOILETS None on route
ORDNANCE SURVEY MAPS Explorer 172 (Chiltern Hills East) and Landranger 175 (Reading & Windsor)

Memorial stone in Hodgemoor Wood

poles that waymark the route as it wanders deeper and deeper into lovely woodland.

The way through the wood divides many times and is crossed by numerous other paths, making left and right directions difficult to follow with certainty. But the route throughout continues to be waymarked, and this is the surest guide.

part of the waymarked path comes out to meet a bridleway. Turn left and soon go past a woodland compound, just beyond which the bridleway forks. Branch left.

At the next track junction, **A** turn left again and, when it next forks, keep left one more time.

Further on, the waymarked Coppice Trail leaves the bridleway by turning right and shortly crosses a prominent track. Keep an eye open for the yellow-banded

Continue beyond a wooden barrier to rejoin a bridleway **B**.

Eventually the waymarked route does lead back to the car park at the start.

> **?** *In Hodgemoor Wood there is a memorial stone. Who is it dedicated to?*

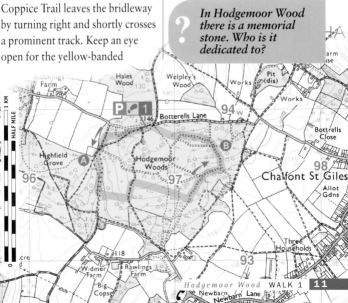

2 *Great Kimble*

START Little Kimble

DISTANCE 2 miles (3.2km)

TIME 1½ hours

PARKING Little Kimble Station

ROUTE FEATURES Farm fields, stiles, steps, railway crossing, some ascent

This short walk, based on the quiet village of Kimble and a short stretch of the Ridgeway National Trail, is a good introduction to the many beauties of the Chiltern Hills. Beautiful beech woodlands make their presence felt, but so too do the rolling farmlands of the area.

Leave the station and turn right, soon entering an enclosed path running alongside the railway line. At a stile, enter a field and follow the right-hand edge to another stile in the far corner (ignore an intermediate stile on the right).

Go forward along another enclosed path which leads up steps to a road. Turn right, crossing the railway bridge and immediately go left down steps so that you are parallel to the railway line once more.

Two more stiles lead across a small paddock into a large arable field. Keep to the left-hand field margin, as far as a metal kissing-gate on the left. Through this, cross the railway line with great care.

In the next field, bear right along a grassy path to a stile in the far corner and then go up the next field alongside a small, elongated pond on the left, to a corner.

Ⓐ Cross a stile and bear half-right, aiming for the right-hand edge of a red-brick house in the distance.

PUBLIC TRANSPORT Bus and rail services to start

REFRESHMENTS Pub in Great Kimble

PUBLIC TOILETS None on route

ORDNANCE SURVEY MAPS Explorer 181 (Chiltern Hills North) and Landranger 165 (Aylesbury & Leighton Buzzard)

Beside the house, a stile gives on to an access driveway leading out to the A4010.

Cross the road with care and go on to a broad track opposite, but immediately bear right, along a branching track into scrub.

The track leads out to a road (Cadsdean Road). Turn left and follow the road for about ¼ mile (400m), taking care against approaching traffic.

Continue to a path on the left, signposted for the Ridgeway **B**. Leave the road here, through a kissing-gate, and start up a long flight of steps, ending at another gate into a large field.

Go forward across the field and, on the far side, enter a short stretch of scrub before intercepting a bridleway.

Keep following the Ridgeway footpath, which immediately goes through a gate and continues as a broad, grassy path along the bottom edge of Pulpit Hill.

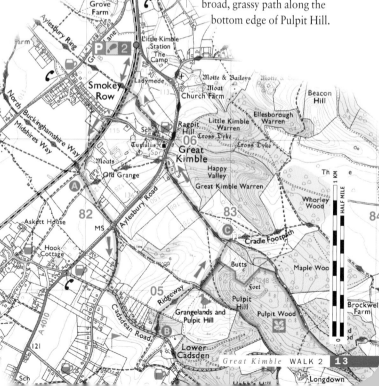

Great Kimble WALK 2

After a short section of open pasture, the Ridgeway path climbs to another gate and rises a little farther to meet a sunken bridleway **C**. Turn left (signposted to Wolverton).

Go down the bridleway, which is flanked by beech, hawthorn, ivy, sycamore and field maple. The descending track becomes a surfaced lane, leading out to the A4010.

Turn right and cross the road with care, passing the Church of St Nicholas.

Bridleway, Great Kimble

Just within the churchyard of **St Nicholas' Church** is a lovely sign depicting the patron saint of children. The church itself is 14th century, but was substantially modified in Victorian times.

After the church, at the Bernard Arms, turn left into Church Lane.

Immediately on reaching Great Kimble School, turn right along a signposted path leading across a narrow enclosure. In the next field, bear left and cross to the right-hand edge of the field.

The Bernard Arms has hosted some important guests in its time. Formerly known as the Chequers, it has been visited by a number of Prime Ministers, including Harold Wilson, and John Major who turned up for a drink with Boris Yeltsin, the Russian President.

Follow a waymarked route across small enclosures and pass a large fish-filled pond before crossing a stream.

Go forward across the next field to a stile on the other side giving on to a railway crossing. Ignore this and turn right along the field boundary, retracing the outward route to Little Kimble Station. ●

In 1635 John Hampden led a protest meeting in Great Kimble against a new tax. Can you discover what the tax was?

Black Park Country Park

Black Park is a truly fascinating mixed woodland; a great diversity of trees are found here, from Scots pine to beautiful beeches and oaks. A sculpture trail takes visitors around the park, but greater interest lies in the part the park has played in film epics.

START Black Park
DISTANCE 2½ miles (4km)
TIME 1½ hours
PARKING Pay-and-display car park at entrance on Black Park Road
ROUTE FEATURES Woodland trails, lakeside paths

3

Leave the car park by heading along a broad track to reach the lake. Turn right.

Walk around the lake edge to the Visitor Centre, and, just past the centre, turn right on to a broad woodland track.

Follow this until, at a track junction, a large wooden sculpture is encountered nearby. Here, turn left Ⓐ.

When the continuing track forks, branch right, passing a cleared, grassy area. At the next track

Hagrid's Cottage, Black Park

PUBLIC TRANSPORT Buses to Iver Heath and Wexham Street
REFRESHMENTS Café at Visitor Centre
PUBLIC TOILETS Adjoining Visitor Centre
ORDNANCE SURVEY MAPS Explorer 172 (Chiltern Hills East) and Landranger 175 (Reading & Windsor)

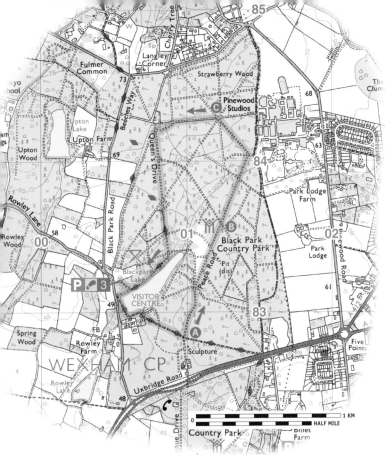

junction, keep ahead on a long drive flanked by pine trees.

Keep ahead at the next junction, too, along Peace Road **B**.

Keep going forward at the next junction, too, soon crossing a stream. Follow the track as it leads around the woodland, eventually to reach Five Points Crossroads.

> ▢ **Black Park** has featured in a number of film epics. Close by the cleared area, a 'stone' cottage was built: this was Hagrid's Cottage from the film *Harry Potter*. The woodland on the right of the Peace Road was also used in one of the original *Star Wars* trilogy.

C Take the second turning on the left, which immediately forks. Keep left.

Black Park Lake

? *Near the lake you find something dedicated to the memory of 'A Great Bloke' What is it and who was he?*

At the next path junction, turn left and at the following one go left once more on to a long, straight track.

Keep going forward, ignoring side-turnings. When the main track swings to the right, leave it, keeping ahead alongside a wooden fence, on a path that leads to the lake.

Walk along the lakeside path as far as the outflow. Here, turn right to return to the car park. ●

A sculpture in Black Park

4 Hughenden Manor and Millfield Wood

START Hughenden
DISTANCE 2½ miles (4km)
TIME 1½ hours
PARKING South Lodge (A4128)
ROUTE FEATURES Parkland, woodland, some ascent

Hughenden will forever be associated with Benjamin Disraeli, Prime Minister from 1874 until 1880, who lived at the manor and is buried in the nearby churchyard. The walk visits the manor-house, now a National Trust property, before climbing into Millfield Wood Nature Reserve.

Begin from a small car park near the lodge at the southern end of the park, and follow a surfaced path to a small bridge, passing some substantial cedars.

Cross the bridge spanning a stream and go forward across parkland to connect with a grassy avenue bordered by young lime trees. Turn right and follow the avenue to another lodge.

At the lodge, divert right to a kissing-gate and then walk around the lodge boundary to rejoin the path.

The path leads up to wrought-iron gates giving into the grounds of the manor. Again, turn right, through a kissing-gate, and then forward to intercept the main drive at a gate.

A Turn left and follow the drive up to the manor.

Go back down the driveway, crossing a cattle-grid to reach the

> **?** *What can you take, what can you leave and what can you kill in Millfield Wood?*

PUBLIC TRANSPORT Buses to Hughenden
REFRESHMENTS Tearoom at Hughenden Manor (seasonal opening)
PUBLIC TOILETS At start
ORDNANCE SURVEY MAPS Explorer 172 (Chiltern Hills East), Landranger 165 (Aylesbury & Leighton Buzzard)

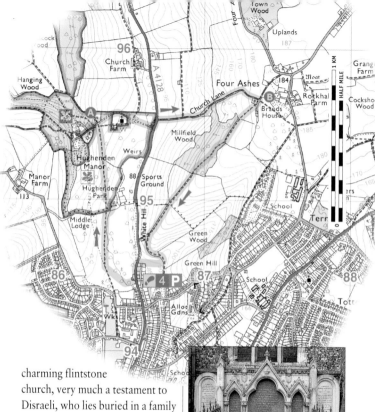

charming flintstone church, very much a testament to Disraeli, who lies buried in a family vault below the east window.

From the church, continue down the drive to meet the main road and there turn left.

After about 40 yds (36m), cross the road with great care to enter a signposted bridleway opposite, an old 'church road' that would have been used by people in isolated farmsteads to get to the church.

The bridleway climbs between a

The Disraeli family vault

Hughenden Manor was purchased by Disraeli in 1848, long before he became Prime Minister. It was originally built to a Georgian design but was altered to its present Gothic state after 1860. The house contains many of Disraeli's effects, including labels sent to him by Queen Victoria. (The manor and gardens are closed Nov–Feb incl., tel. 01494 755573, infoline 755565.)

Hughenden Manor

At the bottom of the field, bear left to another stile giving on to a path along the top edge of Millfield Wood.

Continue down through the woodland. On reaching a National Trust sign, bear right, continuing to descend to reach a collection of gates. Here, bear half-right towards houses, crossing rough pasture and passing an area of new tree plantings to reach a metal kissing-gate giving on to the A4128.

fence and hedgerow and later becomes a sunken track (known as a holloway) flanked by ivy-laden hazel and hawthorn, to reach Millfield Wood Nature Reserve.

B At the top of the climb, turn right over a stile into Millfield and cross to another stile opposite. Over this, turn right and go down the next field, keeping to the right-hand field edge.

Take care emerging on to the road (there is no footpath) and turn left to return to the car park. ●

Hughenden Church

Millfield Wood is a rare example of semi-natural Chiltern beechwood growing on chalk, and an SSSI. The wood, which has many tall beeches, also has ash and wild cherry, and an understorey of hazel, holly, field maple and whitebeam. Unlike most beechwoods it has many flowers, with quite a few indicator species of ancient woodland (goldilocks buttercup, wood anemone, coral root, wood barley and herb Paris), as well as the more common bluebell, dog's mercury and lily of the valley.

West Wycombe Hill

West Wycombe Hill is the site of an Iron Age hillfort established about 2,500 years ago. The hill, a piece of chalk downland interspersed with mature woodland, was a defended settlement and probably a local centre for trade.

START West Wycombe
DISTANCE 2½ miles (4km)
TIME 1½ hours
PARKING Car park (free) on Chorley Road (start)
ROUTE FEATURES Woodland tracks and paths, some ascent, steps

5

On West Wycombe Hill

Leave the car park and cross the road on to a footpath signposted to the 'Caves'. Cross an intermediate path and, when the track forks, bear right (signposted), walking across a hill slope to meet a road. Turn left.

Soon reach the Hell Fire Caves ⒶA on the left (at the time of writing open Nov–Feb: Sat & Sun & bank holidays and Mar–Oct: daily 11.00–17.30). The caves were named by Sir Francis Dashwood, who founded the notorious Hellfire Club in about 1755, a distraction for 'gentlemen' of wealth and position.

> **?** *West Wycombe Hill is populated by roe deer. See if you can spot any. A quiet approach is best. When are they most likely to be seen?*

PUBLIC TRANSPORT Buses to West Wycombe
REFRESHMENTS Café in garden centre at start, pubs in West Wycombe
PUBLIC TOILETS Garden centre
ORDNANCE SURVEY MAPS Explorer 172 (Chiltern Hills East) and Landranger 165 (Aylesbury & Leighton Buzzard)

Go up steps to the right of the caves and, at the top, continue climbing a broad, grassy track to the flint-built, hexagonal Dashwood Mausoleum, which dates from 1764–5 and is still used for family burials.

> Built in 1761, the location of **St Lawrence's Church** within an Iron Age hillfort, was almost certainly a deliberate attempt to Christianise a pagan site.

Keep to the left of the mausoleum and, when the path divides, branch right and follow a wall to reach a church.

Leave the churchyard at a gate and go across a car park,

shortly bearing left towards a row of low bollards to reach a broad track.

Follow the track, left, as it heads through beech, hazel, yew, holly and oak woodland and scrub, with lovely views of the hills to the west.

When the track forks, branch right and continue as far as a cross-path **B**, with a waymark pole indicating the course of the 'Circular Walk Path'. Ignore this and turn right.

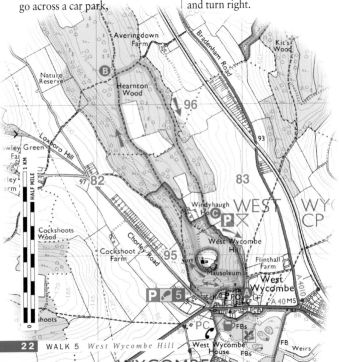

About 200 yds (183m) after the right turn, keep an eye open for a path on the right heading into the woodland. It is not especially clear, but there is an indistinct waymark arrow on a nearby tree. The path starts about 30 yds (27m) before the main path reaches a field fence – seen ahead.

Turn right on to the path, which is narrow, and descend. The rock underlying the path is flint, which can be slippery when wet.

Meandering agreeably through the woodland, the path is seasonally masked by fallen leaves. As a guide, it roughly parallels the left-hand boundary of the woodland.

Finally, the path emerges into the top corner of a large sloping pasture. Keep forward alongside a mature hedgerow of field maple, blackthorn, ivy and hazel.

After about 150 yds (137m), turn back into the woodland at a stile **C** (collapsed at the time of writing) and immediately bear left.

The path eventually emerges at a road. Cross to a path opposite and follow this across a field towards the mausoleum.

In front of the mausoleum, turn left down the grassy path used earlier in the walk. After about 100 yds (91m), leave the main track by turning right on to a branching path going down steps.

At the bottom of the steps, keep right, descending on a path that leads back to the car park. ●

St Lawrence's Church, West Wycombe Hill

6 *Marlow and the Thames*

Marlow is a hugely attractive town with its own rowing regatta and a history that goes back beyond the 'Domesday Book'; it is a lively, buzzing place and a perfect spot from which to begin an easy walk along the Thames Path.

START Marlow
DISTANCE 3 miles (4.8km)
TIME 1½ hours
PARKING Pound Lane pay-and-display car park, Marlow
ROUTE FEATURES Riverside path, gates, stiles, farm tracks

The Thames at Marlow

Leave the car park and turn right, heading towards the centre of Marlow. At the main entrance to Higginson Park (or earlier), turn into the park and follow a diagonal path to reach the Thames. Turn right.

Eventually the surfaced Thames-side path breaks out into a large open meadow. Simply keep heading in the same direction, walking alongside the river.

Continue upriver passing modern housing built on Temple Mill

PUBLIC TRANSPORT Buses to Marlow
REFRESHMENTS Cafés, pubs and restaurants in Marlow
PUBLIC TOILETS Higginson Park (near start)
PLAY AREA Higginson Park
ORDNANCE SURVEY MAPS Explorer 172 (Chiltern Hills East), Landranger 175 (Reading & Windsor)

Island – named after the Templars – and a short way on, as a weir is approached, leave the Thames Path by turning inland along a track  **Ⓐ** leading towards Low Grounds Farm.

At a double bend, leave the track by branching right on to a rough farm track heading back towards Marlow **Ⓑ**.

Beyond a gate and stile, the track improves and soon becomes surfaced. Keep forward to a T-junction. Turn right to return to the car park. ●

Lovely buildings lie along the riverbank on the opposite side – **Bisham church** is especially well-sited, as is the abbey – founded by the Knights Templar – a little further along.

How many coots you can spot along this stretch of the Thames? They are black with a white patch on their head. Where might the expression 'bald as a coot' have come from?

7 *Leygrove's Wood*

START Cadmore End
DISTANCE 3 miles (4.8km)
TIME 1½–2 hours
PARKING Car park at start
ROUTE FEATURES Woodland trails, farmland tracks, some ascent

This is a serene and gentle walk that ambles through the beautiful woodland north of Cadmore End. The views from the high point of the walk, of gently sloping farmland bordered by trees and hedgerows, are lovely.

Leave the car park by heading down a track towards the nearby motorway. The track passes beneath the motorway and emerges on the other side into beech woodland.

Continue to follow the track, which shortly bears right and descends to cross a neck of open farmland, before re-entering woodland Ⓐ.

About 40 yds (36m) farther on, leave the broad track by turning left on to an initially grassy path into mixed woodland of hazel, larch, lodgepole pine, beech and rowan.

At first, the route is not well waymarked, but soon acquires white directional arrows, painted on tree trunks. Keep forward through the woodland, ignoring branching tracks. Continue as far as a track junction, and here,

> *Can you spot any bullfinches? The mixed woodlands on this walk are favoured by bullfinches, a lovely bird: the male has a vivid red breast and black cap.*

PUBLIC TRANSPORT Buses to Cadmore End (to start)
REFRESHMENTS Pubs in Cadmore End and along B482
PUBLIC TOILETS None on route
ORDNANCE SURVEY MAPS Explorer 171 (Chiltern Hills West) and Landranger 175 (Reading & Windsor)

Leygrove's Wood is a habitat favoured by many birds, especially pheasant, which scurry about in the undergrowth alarmingly. There are two subspecies of male pheasant to look out for, which are identical except that one has a broad white collar.

leaving the broad track, go forward on to a path (identified on a nearby tree as path S51) **B**.

The path descends gently through the woodland. Follow it as it climbs to the woodland edge, there emerging into farmland.

Go forward, keeping to the left of a hedgerow, and follow this to

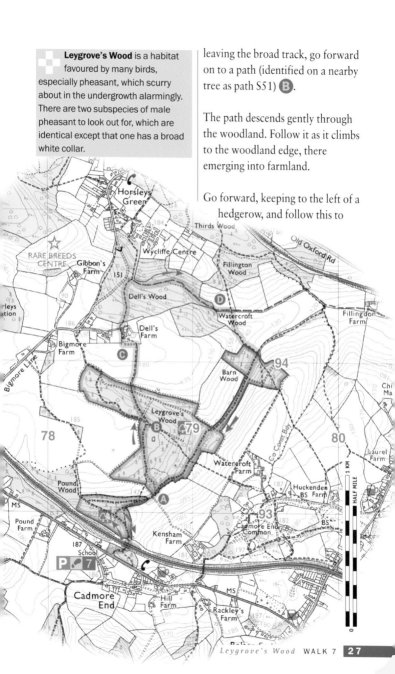

the boundary of Dell's Farm, part of the Kensham Farm estate.

Turn left alongside the farmstead boundary **C**, turning right after 100 yds (91m) on to a broad, grassy track leading to a farm access.

Walk along the access until it bends left, and there leave it by going through a metal kissing-gate.

Cross the ensuing pasture, walking half-right to a metal gate giving into Dell's Wood, a beautiful stand of beech woodland.

It may not be unusual to spot a hunting **buzzard** patrolling the skies or, more likely, a **red kite**. The latter, particularly, are now becoming quite well established in the Chiltern hills.

In the wood, bear right on a path which soon becomes waymarked and leads to a narrow, surfaced lane.

On reaching the lane, immediately leave it by turning right on to a signposted bridleway.

Farmland near Leygrove's Wood

In Leygrove's Wood

A waymarked route leads on through more woodland and, eventually, reaches a wooden gate and barrier, giving access to a lovely scene of undulating farmland, fringed by copses and hedgerows **D**.

Go forward along the line of an old fence. After about 80 yds (73m), look for a waymark pole in the fenceline on the right. Here, leave the continuing path and turn sharply right, climbing the adjacent field and aiming for the left-hand end of a hedgerow at the top.

From the top of the climb, where the views are stunning, go downhill, alongside a well-established hedgerow, to a field corner.

In the corner, pass a dilapidated stile and turn right on to footpath S52.

At a crosspath, keep forward past a barrier with a 'No Horses' sign on it and soon reach a broad track bearing left.

The track eventually completes the circle, rejoining the outward route. When it does so, keep forward to the woodland edge and across the neck of farmland to return along the broad track that leads back beneath the motorway to the car park where the walk started. ●

8 *Hambleden*

START Hambleden
DISTANCE 3½ miles (5.6km)
TIME 1½–2 hours
PARKING Car park at Hambleden
ROUTE FEATURES Woodland trails, farm tracks, roads, stiles, steps

Hambleden is an idyllic village: a setting for film versions of novels, the birthplace of barons, noblemen and bishops. This is one of the prettiest villages in Britain, with a Jacobean manor house, village green with pump and chestnut tree, delightful old cottages and a beautiful church.

From the 'Visitors' car park, turn right on to a gently rising lane, which becomes steeper as it passes Kenricks, and ascends into woodland, climbing through a copse of young sycamore, field maple and ash.

As the gradient relents, keep forward alongside a lovely row of beech trees and, at the top edge of the woodland, go forward on to a field edge track.

At a track junction **A**, turn left towards Hutton's Farm. On reaching the farm, branch left on to

Kenricks is the former rectory of Hambleden village, built on the site of the house that was the birthplace of St Thomas de Cantelupe, Chancellor of England in the 13th century and later Bishop of Hereford. The village was used in the filming of *A Village Affair* by Joanna Trollope and in TV adaptations of the *Just William* stories by Richmal Crompton. W.H. Smith, the founder of the bookseller lived in Hambleden and is buried in the village churchyard.

Can you find two children riding on a turtle's back, swimming above fish?

PUBLIC TRANSPORT Buses to Hambleden
REFRESHMENTS Pub and shop in Hambleden
PUBLIC TOILETS None on route
ORDNANCE SURVEY MAPS Explorer 171 (Chiltern Hills West) and Landranger 175 (Reading & Windsor)

Wild clematis seed heads

a broad, grassy track that leads to another farm track.

Go briefly left and then branch right when the track forks, and walk alongside a hedgerow at the top edge of the field, with a lovely view across the valley to the wooded hills opposite.

Hambleden church

Approaching Rockwell End, keep to the right of fence enclosures to locate a stile giving on to a road.

Turn left, and when the road forks, branch right, and right again at the next junction, but only as far as a signposted footpath on the left, about 40 yds (36m) away.

C Here, turn left along a broad field track which, eventually, is flanked by coppiced hazel, field maple, holly and beech, and forms a lovely avenue between farm fields.

Eventually, the track decreases in size and descends into woodland, which contains a few yew trees. Just after a double bend, leave the main descending path by turning left on to a path that parallels the top left-hand edge of the woodland.

Continue to follow the path, always with the woodland edge in sight, but keep an eye open for an indistinct path branching right **D**. This descends to meet a road at

The track soon enters woodland. Here, bear right and, when the main track bears left, leave it by turning right, on to a narrow path, waymarked by white arrows painted on trees.

The path roughly parallels the top edge of the woodland and soon enters a long, thin strip of woodland. Keep an eye open here for a fallen beech tree showing the perfectly circular holes made by woodpeckers. Look out, too, for a path branching left, about 100 yds (91m) before the woodland edge at a road **B**.

Turn left (waymark on tree) to the edge of a large arable field. Strike across the field. The path is not always evident, but aim to the right of buildings at Rockwell End in the distance.

Pheasant's Hill, at a footpath sign. Take care emerging on to the road. (The branching path in the woodland is not clear, especially in autumn when the paths are lost beneath leaves, nor is there any waymarking. If it is missed, simply continue going down through the woodland, maintaining the same direction, to reach a road just beyond a large barrier. Turn right at the road and walk along it to Pheasant's Hill, and there turn right into Bottom Hill, walking uphill for a short distance to meet the correct route emerging from the woodland at a footpath sign.)

Cross the road and go down steps opposite and along a very narrow path, flanked by holly. At the end of the path go forward, but only as far as a cross-path, signposted for the Chiltern Way. Turn left.

The continuing path runs between gardens to a gate and then continues alongside a fence to a stile and gate, giving into a large field.

Cross two fields, bearing right in the second to reach a road. Turn left, walking towards the village church.

Keep left and walk through the centre of the village, past the Stag and Huntsman pub to return to the car park. ●

Woodland trail in the Hambleden valley

● Ancient church ● poet's monument ● woodpeckers

9 *Stoke Poges*

START Stoke Poges
DISTANCE 3½ miles (5.6km)
TIME 2 hours
PARKING Car park near St Giles' Church
ROUTE FEATURES Fields, roads, golf course, stiles

The area around Stoke Poges is forever linked with the name of Thomas Gray (1716–71), whose poem 'Elegy Written in a Country Churchyard' is one of the best known in English literature. Gray wrote the poem in the churchyard of St Giles, where he now lies buried. This walk takes a brief tour around the countryside he loved.

St Giles' Church dates from Saxon times, though there are much later additions. Thomas Gray is buried in a family vault outside the east window, but his name does not appear – there was insufficient room. Outside the entrance is the yew where Gray is said to have been inspired to create his most famous work 'Elegy Written in a Country Churchyard'.

🥾 Leave the car park and cross the road with care (blind bend) to walk along the signposted lane to the churchyard. The walk turns right at the second lychgate, but first take time to visit the church.

From the lichgate, walk into Gray's Field and turn right to visit the huge monument to Gray.

Continue across the field to a kissing-gate giving on to a road. Cross with care into the field opposite and walk along the left-hand field margin.

? *Green woodpeckers favour the open but partially wooded 'countryside' of a golf course. They are often seen at Wexham Park. See if you can spot any. When are they not so 'green'?*

PUBLIC TRANSPORT Buses to Stoke Poges
REFRESHMENTS Pubs in Stoke Poges
PUBLIC TOILETS None on route
ORDNANCE SURVEY MAPS Explorer 172 (Chiltern Hills East) and Landranger 175 (Reading & Windsor)

At the next gate, bear half-right on a grassy path to a gate giving on to a busy road, near a road junction.

Cross into Farthing Green Lane and follow the lane for about 600 yds (549m), as far as a signposted bridleway on the right, an oak- and hawthorn-bordered path along the boundary of a golf course.

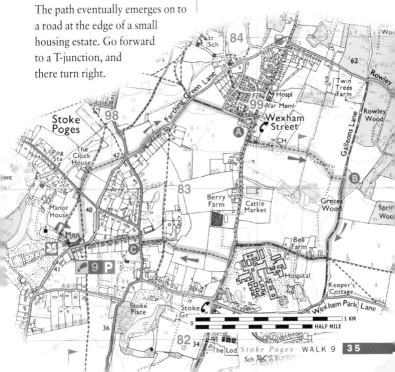

Thomas Gray memorial

The path eventually emerges on to a road at the edge of a small housing estate. Go forward to a T-junction, and there turn right.

A Walk down the road for 125 yds (114m) until just before the entrance to Wexham Park Golf Course. Turn left on to a sign-posted footpath alongside houses, leading to a stile giving on to the golf course grounds.

Go through the car park, passing the clubhouse to reach a driving range. Here keep ahead on to a

Lychgate, St Giles' Church

broad track across the golf course (keep an eye open for flying golf balls on crossing the course).

When the track across the course bears sharply right, leave it by crossing a fairway to a stile with yellow paint on it, directly opposite but partly concealed in a hedgerow.

B Beyond the stile, turn right along a wooded path and continue as far as a metal gate on the right, close by a large barn-like building. Here a footpath crosses the bridleway. Turn right over the stile and follow the footpath to a surfaced driveway beyond.

Walk along the driveway to meet a road, near the entrance to a hospital. Turn left, crossing the road when it is safe to do so.

After about 100 yds (91m), leave the roadside path by turning right, over a stile and heading straight across the ensuing field.

Cross into the next field and go forward along the left-hand edge to a concealed and boggy ditch in a corner, the worst of which can be avoided on the right. Cross a stile and head half-right across a small paddock to a stile giving on to a lane.

Turn left along the lane and walk out to a main road. Turn right, crossing the road, and shortly turn left into Duffield Park **C**.

Continue forward along a gravel track and go through a metal kissing-gate to the right of Barton Spinney. Walk along a path maintaining the same direction, crossing a number of house driveways until, at a final kissing-gate, the path emerges on to a road.

Cross to the path opposite and walk back to the entrance of the car park before crossing the road again. ●

Watlington Park

START Christmas Common
DISTANCE 3½ miles (5.6km)
TIME 2 hours
PARKING Car park at start
ROUTE FEATURES Woodland trails, roads, stiles, some ascent

10

The beechwoods of Watlington Park are believed to be of ancient origin, although today's trees have been felled and replanted many times. This walk makes an easy tour of Watlington Hill and Park, and involves a modest degree of ascent.

Leave the car park at its far right-hand corner, on to a track beside a field flanked by beech trees.

Watlington Hill

Rising above the beech woodlands of Watlington Park, **Watlington Hill** attains 699ft (213m). It consists of skeletal soil chalk downland, scrub and beech copses, and provides impressive views over the adjacent countryside. More than 30 species of butterfly favour this area, notably marbled white, comma, chalk hill blue and dark green fritillary. Keep an eye open, too, for birdsfoot trefoil, bee orchid, wild candy tuft and, in autumn, the bright pink seed heads of the spindle tree. Found along the hill slopes are yews, rare in the Chilterns.

Just after a kissing-gate the path forks. Branch right (waymark). The continuing path is a long, steady

PUBLIC TRANSPORT Buses to Christmas Common
REFRESHMENTS Pub at Christmas Common
PUBLIC TOILETS None on route
ORDNANCE SURVEY MAPS Explorer 171 (Chiltern Hills West) and Landranger 175 (Reading & Windsor)

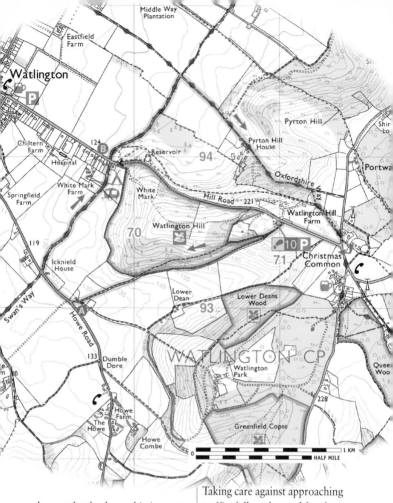

descent that leads to a kissing-gate and stile beyond, following a sunken track around the base of Watlington Hill.

Eventually, the path comes down to meet a farm track **A**. Turn right, walk out to a road and turn right again.

Taking care against approaching traffic, follow the road for about 300 yds (274m). Leave the road by turning right on to a section of the

> **?** *Red kites are a common feature soaring above the Chiltern countryside. Do you know where they were reintroduced from?*

Ridgeway Path, directly opposite the entrance to Dame Alice Farm.

Continue on a broad track, which later intercepts a road **B**. Cross into the continuing track opposite, still following the Ridgeway Path, here also part of the Icknield Way.

Keep on to reach a surfaced lane and here turn right, leaving the Ridgeway Path for the Oxfordshire Way.

When the road surfacing ends, keep forward on a rising field track, climbing steadily into the edge of woodland.

Just as the rising path becomes enclosed by fences, leave it by turning right over a stile in a field corner. Follow a path, bearing right, around and across a field to run alongside a tall hawthorn hedgerow.

The path finally emerges on to a road. Turn right and, a few strides on, turn right again for Watlington. Follow this for nearly ¼ mile (400m) to return to the car park. ●

Woodland track, Watlington Park

11

Ellesborough and Chequers

This gentle walk explores the countryside around Chequers, the Prime Minister's country retreat. Coombe Hill, highest of the Chiltern Hills, rises to the east, and everywhere snatches of beech woodland are a delight to wander in.

START Ellesborough
DISTANCE 3½ miles (5.6km)
TIME 2 hours
PARKING Roadside layby west of Ellesborough
ROUTE FEATURES Woodland trails, farm fields, stiles

The **Church of St Peter and St Paul** has been a place of worship for many Prime Ministers, and although most of the building is Victorian, there has been a church in this lovely elevated position above its village for centuries.

Begin from a small layby parking area along Ellesborough road, walking back towards the village, with care, and, opposite the church, turn right on to a signposted footpath.

After about 200 yds (183m), leave the rising track by turning left at a signposted path on the left, giving into a large field, across which there is a clear path.

On the far side of the field, the track emerges at a road. Turn right for about 100 yds (91m) and then left at a signposted bridleway, going past houses and climbing into the edge of woodland along the lower slopes of Coombe Hill.

The Chiltern woodlands are renowned for their beeches, but ash, with its black buds, occurs here, too. See if you can find any along this walk.

PUBLIC TRANSPORT Buses to Ellesborough
REFRESHMENTS Pub at Butler's Cross
PUBLIC TOILETS None on route
ORDNANCE SURVEY MAPS Explorer 181 (Chiltern Hills North) and Landranger 165 (Aylesbury & Leighton Buzzard)

At a track junction **Ⓐ**, just before the entrance to the Coombe Hill estate, turn right on a track that wanders agreeably along to emerge at a road, opposite North Park Lodge.

Turn left, and left again on the road to Dunsmore. After 30 yds (27m), leave it by turning right at a barrier. Take the right-hand of a number of tracks and follow a leafy bridleway.

Coombe Hill from Ellesborough

Continue to a prominent track junction, meeting the Ridgeway **B**. Turn right, descending, and walk down to rejoin the road.

> **Chequers** has been the country residence of Prime Ministers since 1921, when Lord Lee of Fareham gave it to the nation in the hope that '... the high and pure air of the Chiltern hills and woods will ... benefit the nation as well as its chosen leaders'.

Ridgeway by bearing right on a field-edge path around the edge of Whorley Wood.

The path leads to a stile beside a gate. Go forward,

Cross to a kissing-gate opposite and bear left on a field path with Chequers in the distance. Walk across the main driveway to Chequers, then a narrow enclosure, before heading across a field to Maple Wood in the distance.

At the woodland boundary, turn right, following its edge, with good views of Chequers, to another kissing-gate. Here, leave the

crossing a track, along a path that soon emerges into open pasture. Here bear left on a broad field path.

On the far side, the path goes down steps into Ellesborough Warren. A brief woodland interlude leads to a clear path across the slopes of Beacon Hill.

Head for a stile in a field corner, beyond which a grassy path leads towards the village of Ellesborough, with the church prominent on its roadside knoll.

Ellesborough church

Rejoin the road at a kissing-gate and turn left to return to the starting point of the walk, taking care against the approaching traffic on the busy road. ●

● Woodland ● attractive village ● ancient church ● sunken lanes

Little Missenden

START Little Missenden
DISTANCE 3¾ miles (6km)
TIME 2–2½ hours
PARKING Roadside parking at village green
ROUTE FEATURES Farm tracks, holloways, field paths, some ascent, stiles

12

Unlike many of the surrounding villages, Little Missenden has been largely unaffected by the passage of time. and remains as peaceful and idyllic as ever, a charming example of the true English village. This walk climbs high above the village, making use on the ascent and descent of ancient trackways.

🥾 Walk past the green and out of the village. Go past the Crown Inn, and, at a road bend 50 yds (46m) farther on, turn right on to a footpath signposted for the South Bucks Way. This continues as a broad track parallel with the River Missenden, along which there used to be a number of watermills.

Signpost, Little Missenden

> The **Church of St John the Baptist** is famous for its wall-paintings, dating from the 13th century. The church itself is Saxon (AD 950–1050) and uses Roman bricks in its chancel arch.

When the broad track swings left towards a farm, leave it by going forward over a stile and along the right-hand edge of an elongated field.

At the next stile, the track meets another. This is Mop End Lane **A**. Turn right, climbing now on an enclosed

PUBLIC TRANSPORT Buses to Little Missenden
REFRESHMENTS Pubs in Little Missenden
PUBLIC TOILETS None on route
PLAY AREA Children's playground at start
ORDNANCE SURVEY MAPS Explorer 172 (Chiltern Hills East) and Landranger 165 (Aylesbury & Leighton Buzzard)

The men who worked in the woods to make chair legs had a special name, beginning with the letter 'B'. Can you discover what it was?

The **chalk and clay hills** that surround the village have long been a source of timber, particularly beechwood, for chair-making. The chair-makers worked deep in the woods making chair legs until the outbreak of the First World War. In spring, the woodlands are bright with bluebells and orchids.

pathway flanked by lovely hedgerows of hazel, field maple, blackthorn, beech and the occasional ash.

The track climbs steadily for a while before levelling off as it runs alongside farm fields.

Continue to follow the track as far as Mop End Farm. Here the track emerges on to a surfaced lane. Turn left and, after about 80 yds (73m), leave the lane by turning

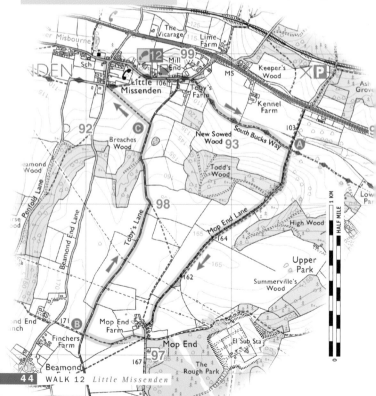

right over a stile at a signposted footpath.

Keep to the right-hand edge of the ensuing field (ignoring a path heading diagonally across the field). Continue to a stile in a hedge corner and, beyond it, cross the next field to a step-stile giving on to another track 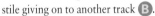.

Cottages, Little Missenden

Turn right (Toby's Lane), to follow another delightful old track. Go down this for some distance to a stile on the left  giving access to a sloping pasture across which a path descends towards Little Missenden.

Go left and down the field. At the bottom, cross a stile and turn right into the village. At a T-junction, turn left to visit the church – one of the oldest in the Chilterns.

Return from the church and follow the main village road back to the green.

Mop End Lane, Little Missenden

13 *Stonor*

START Stonor
DISTANCE 4 miles (6.4km)
TIME 2 hours
PARKING Roadside at start
ROUTE FEATURES Woodland trails, roads, farm fields, stiles

The area of the Chiltern Hills around Stonor is so wonderfully peaceful and tranquil, a place where walkers can find solitude among the folds and hollows of the countryside. This walk goes through Stonor Deer Park to the hamlet of Southend before finding a way back along ancient farm lanes.

Go through a tall kissing-gate into Stonor Deer Park, along a footpath signposted for Southend and the Chiltern Way. Go forward on a rising grassy path to walk alongside a deer fence.

Stonor House, a lovely building, appears in the valley below, and soon the path levels and contours across a hill slope.

The fence-side path leads to a tall gate at the edge of mixed woodland **A**. Go forward on a waymarked path to meet a broad track bearing right and leading out

Stonor House is so well concealed that during the days of religious persecution its Roman Catholic family evaded detection. The Stonor family have been landholders here since before the Norman Conquest, and, if tales are to be believed, more than one of them has died in the house, for it is said to be haunted.

of the woodland to a road near the hamlet of Southend, crossing the Oxfordshire-Buckinghamshire county boundary in the process.

Turn left along the road for 150 yds (137m) and leave it at the next

PUBLIC TRANSPORT Buses to Stonor
REFRESHMENTS Pub in Stonor village
PUBLIC TOILETS None on route
ORDNANCE SURVEY MAPS Explorer 171 (Chiltern Hills West) and Landranger 175 (Reading & Windsor)

> **?** *Trees can be dated by counting the number of rings from their centre out to the bark; one ring equals one year. See if you can find any timber, from which you can work out the age of the tree when it was felled.*

Go forward along a field edge and, on the far side of the field, bear half-left to enter Summerheath Wood.

The way through the wood is waymarked by white arrows painted on trees. When the path forks at a waymark post, branch left to follow the path out to a road, near a junction **B**.

turning on the right (a concrete track). Walk along this for 100 yds (91m) and then turn left, over a stile into a field.

Turn left, ignoring the immediate left turn, and, going past Turville Cottage, continue to follow the road to another road junction.

On a sunny autumn day the view ahead is breathtaking; every shade of gold is present in the trees and hedgerows around Pishill, from the brightest yellow to the most intense russet. Overhead, red kites patrol the skies, scanning the fields for food.

kissing-gate giving on to a partially enclosed track.

C Turn right on to the track, which later follows the edge of a large field and continues into the next, now descending.

Ignore the left turn, but keep forward to a second junction and cross to a signposted path going left past houses to one called Saviours.

Find a path and gate near the entrance to Saviours and then follow a grassy path across two fields. In the third field, cut across an indented left-hand corner to a

At the bottom of the descent, turn left along a broad track and follow this out to a road. Turn right.

Taking care against approaching traffic, follow the road to a junction with the B480. Turn left to return to the starting point of the walk.

Stonor House

Burnham Beeches Nature Reserve

START Farnham Common
DISTANCE 4 miles (6.4km)
TIME 2 hours
PARKING Car park at Farnham Common entrance
ROUTE FEATURES Woodland, farm fields, stiles, a little road walking

14

Burnham Beeches Nature Reserve, comprising 540 acres (220 ha), is owned by the Corporation of London. This walk goes through the reserve, with its ancient woodland, and passes Dorney Wood, the official country residence of the Chancellor of the Exchequer.

Burnham Beeches is one of the foremost wood pastures in Britain, areas where ancient trees and grazing animals occur together. The old pollarded trees are particularly valuable because they support many rare and declining insects and fungi, which are found only in such ancient trees.

From the car park, walk along the main drive to an information panel at Victory Cross. Here turn right, soon passing a barrier and bearing left on to Halse Drive.

Keep forward across the end of Victoria Drive and, at a track junction near Hartley Court Moat, take the middle of three tracks.

The track runs out to meet a road. Cross it and go forward into the Portman Burtley estate, bearing right on a woodland track.

At a meeting with a permissive path **A**, keep forward (ignoring the permissive route) and descend to meet an enclosed path at a kissing-gate.

At the end of the path, go forward into the next field, keeping to the left-hand boundary.

PUBLIC TRANSPORT Buses to Farnham Common
REFRESHMENTS Pubs in Farnham Common and Littleworth
PUBLIC TOILETS None on route
ORDNANCE SURVEY MAPS Explorer 172 (Chiltern Hills East) and Landranger 176 (West London)

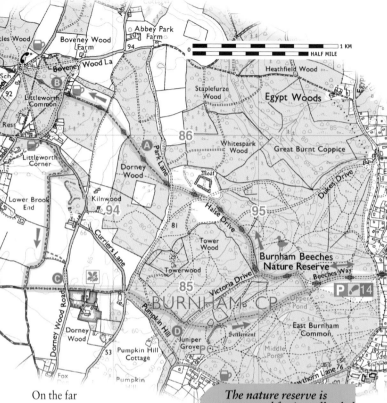

On the far side of the field, stiles lead out to a road, adjacent to the Blackwood Arms pub **B**. Turn left along a wooded lane.

Continue to a crossroads. Turn left and, after about 50 yds (46m), leave the road by turning right over a stile and immediately left along the field boundary.

Follow the field boundary until the path dives left, through a hedge gap, and gives into a large, open field.

The nature reserve is renowned for its pollarded trees, where the branches have been repeatedly cut back at about 8ft (2.4m) above ground to provide timber for stockades and building. See how many examples you can find, both of pollarded oak and beech.

Keep along the field edge and through a hedge gap into the next field. Continue following the field-edge path, until it again turns left through a holly hedgerow.

Stick to the left-hand edge of the ensuing field, on the far side of which the path emerges at a path junction. Here, turn left and walk across a large field to a gate on the far side.

C The gate gives on to a road. Cross to the stile opposite and go forward along the right-hand field boundary.

Keep following the field edge, passing Dorney Wood, and you eventually come out to meet a road.

Here cross to a signboard at the entrance once more to Burnham Beeches Nature Reserve.

Go forward into the reserve on a grassy woodland path, initially roughly parallel with a road on the right. Then it gradually veers away from the road to meet up with other paths and becomes more pronounced. The route descends to cross a track **D** beyond which it climbs for a short while.

The track, which is clear throughout, eventually emerges from the woodland at Victory Cross. Turn left to walk back to the car park. ●

Pollarded oak, Burnham Beeches

15 *Mapledurham and Chazey Wood*

START Mapledurham

DISTANCE 4½ miles (7.2km)

TIME 2 hours

PARKING Mapledurham (limited)

ROUTE FEATURES Mainly surfaced tracks, paths

So enchanting is the village of Mapledurham that it has been used as a setting both for films and television – one of the Inspector Morse episodes was set here. This walk, which begins in the village, is easy and makes a circuit of the lovely Chazey Wood.

Begin from the car park adjoining the church (but please don't park here if there are services in the church) and turn right to walk up through the village. On the way, note the lovely almshouses on the left, which have interesting chimney-pots.

After the last house on the right, turn right on to a bridleway (signposted to Caversham), which goes forward as a surfaced track, to pass Park Farm, and reach a junction near a cottage on the left.

A Turn left and take the next

turning on the right, heading for the mound of Chazey Wood.

The track skirts the woodland boundary before turning into it and emerging on the other side to spend time flirting with an adjacent

> **?** *Ivy is a parasitic plant that attaches itself to a host, which eventually it kills. See if you can find any trees cloaked in ivy.*

PUBLIC TRANSPORT None

REFRESHMENTS None

PUBLIC TOILETS None on route

ORDNANCE SURVEY MAPS Explorer 171 (Chiltern Hills West) and Landranger 175 (Reading & Windsor)

golf course. (Beware of miss-hit golf balls.)

Follow the continuing track to a T-junction near a white, thatched cottage with three chimneys, and here turn right on to a stony track **B**.

When the stony surfacing ends, keep forward along a narrow path sandwiched between sections of Caversham Heath Golf Course.

Continue to follow the path until some modern housing comes into view. About 150 yds (137m) before

Mapledurham Mill

these, look for a path branching right through a hedgerow. Go right here, and along an enclosed path that later turns left to descend a pleasant holloway (a sunken track) flanked by hawthorn, field maple, oak, ash and sycamore.

At the bottom of the holloway, at a T-junction, turn right on to a broad track with riparian farm fields on the left descending to the banks of the River Thames.

The track eventually becomes surfaced again and leads back towards the village of Mapledurham. A good view opens up of Mapledurham House.

Turn left through the village to return to the start.

Mapledurham House, a mellow, red-brick mansion, is one of the largest Elizabethan houses in Oxfordshire, and still the home of the descendants of the original Blount family. Sheltered by the Chiltern Hills, it stands in an idyllic setting beside the Thames. It has an original 16th-century ceiling, a huge oak staircase and a private chapel. The house has literary connections with Alexander Pope, Galsworthy's *Forsyte Saga* and Kenneth Grahame's *Wind in the Willows*. (At time of going to press open Easter–end Sept Sat, Sun & bank hol. Mon 1400–1730. Tel. 01189 723350).

No visit to Mapledurham would be complete without seeing **Mapledurham Mill**, a rare example of a working Thames watermill. It dates from the 16th century and still produces stoneground wholemeal flour. Admission as for house.

Mapledurham House

Ivinghoe Beacon

START Ivinghoe
DISTANCE 4½ miles (7.2km)
TIME 2 hours
PARKING Car park along
B488
ROUTE FEATURES Farm field
paths, uphill section and
steep descent, roads

16

*Ivinghoe Beacon may not be the highest
summit in the Chilterns – that is Coombe
Hill – but it affords a magnificent view
nonetheless, and its ascent can seem quite
demanding on a windy day. This walk
approaches from the south and takes the
easiest line possible.*

Leave the parking space and turn left towards the village of Ivinghoe, taking care against approaching traffic.

After about 100 yds (91m), leave the road by turning right, over a stile (signposted) on to an enclosed path that soon breaks out into an open field. Keep left.

When the left-hand boundary turns

Pitstone Windmill, Ivinghoe

abruptly away, keep forward across a field to a stile. In the next field, bear gradually left to intercept the Ridgeway Path in a field corner **A**.

Turn left on to the Ridgeway, and follow a broad green track as it climbs steadily. Towards the top of the ascent, the path keeps to the left of a gate and contours around the rim of

PUBLIC TRANSPORT Buses to Ivinghoe
REFRESHMENTS Pubs in Ivinghoe
PUBLIC TOILETS None on route
ORDNANCE SURVEY MAPS Explorer 181 (Chiltern Hills North) and Landranger 181
(Aylesbury & Leighton Buzzard)

The summit of **Ivinghoe Beacon**, as its name suggests, was once part of a national network of beacon fires lit to warn of danger, or in celebration. The upper part of the hill is also the site of a Bronze Age hillfort, the ramparts of which can still be made out. The area is rich in archaeological remains, including barrows, enclosure and settlement sites, lynchets, sunken drove roads and dykes.

Incombe Hole before entering a stand of hawthorn scrub.

Emerging from the hawthorns, the path continues as a grassy path and goes on to cross a road. Take the left-hand of two broad tracks

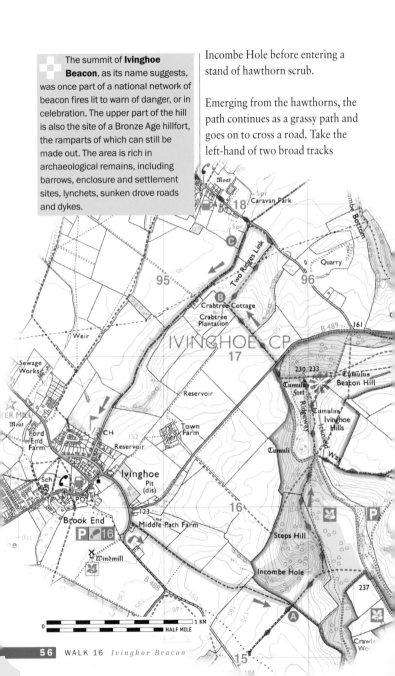

Ivinghoe Beacon

opposite and follow this to the top of Ivinghoe Beacon.

From the top of the hill, go left (west), descending steeply (a place to keep young children in check), to a road. Turn right to a T-junction and right again, as far as a signposted path on the left (cross the road with care), giving into a field.

> **?** Along many of the walks in the Chilterns, wild clematis occurs. It is also called 'Old Man's Beard' from the distinctive beard-like seeds it produces in autumn. See if you can find any.

Go forward along the left-hand edge of an arable field, following an intermittent line of hawthorns. In the next field, walk alongside a fence as far as a waymark on a pole in the fence, and here **B** turn right through ninety degrees and cross undulating pasture, aiming for the tower of Edlesborough church in the distance.

Gradually, drift left to walk alongside a post and wire fence to a kissing-gate giving into the adjoining field. Through this, turn right following the field boundary, which parallels a road. At another gate, emerge briefly on to the roadside.

Turn left along a signposted bridleway, partially surfaced, but at a notice-board for Crab Tree Farmhouse Ⓒ leave the access track by branching right on to a broad, muddy track between hedgerows.

The track, a lovely ancient highway, eventually emerges on to a surfaced road on the edge of Ivinghoe. Go forward, and, at the Rose and Crown pub, turn left into Vicarage Lane.

At the next road junction, near the church, turn left. Go past the

> This walk can be further enhanced by paying a visit to the nearby **Pitstone windmill**, now a National Trust property. Built in 1627, it is thought to be the oldest-surviving post-mill in Britain. A 'post' mill is one where the whole structure turns on a central post, to face into the wind, which explains the cartwheel on its tail. The windmill would be manoeuvred either by manpower or by using a donkey. (Open Jun–Aug, Sun & bank hols 14.30–14.00. Tel. 01494 528051.)

turning to Dunstable and continue along the roadside verge to return to the start. Take care against approaching traffic on crossing to the parking-space. ●

Ivinghoe church

Whiteleaf Hill and Hampden

The great beauty of this walk is the way it peacefully explores lovely beechwoods and ancient tracks. In autumn, the colours are breathtaking; in summer, the woodlands and hedgerows are bright with wild flowers and the trees filled with singing birds.

START Princes Risborough
DISTANCE 4¾ miles (7.6km)
TIME 2–2½ hours
PARKING Car park at Whiteleaf Hill
ROUTE FEATURES Woodland trails, stiles, farm fields, roads

Begin by walking through the Whiteleaf Hill car park to intercept the Ridgeway path. Turn right but, after 200 yds (183m), at a signpost, turn right again on to a bridleway, part of the Icknield Way.

The bridleway runs along the top edge of beech woodland to a path junction. Turn right here, still walking along the woodland boundary, with an open field beyond.

Leave the woodland at a gate, giving on to a broad track (near some radio dishes). Turn left along the woodland boundary, but now outside it.

When the continuing path re-enters woodland **A**, keep forward, descending for a while, and when the path reaches a cross-track, go forward to intercept another. Keep forward again,

> **?** *Many country houses used to have a ditch built in front of them to prevent cattle straying into garden areas but retain the view. One is passed on this walk. See if you can find it. What are they called?*

PUBLIC TRANSPORT Buses to Princes Risborough
REFRESHMENTS Pubs in Princes Risborough
PUBLIC TOILETS None on route
ORDNANCE SURVEY MAPS Explorer 181 (Chiltern Hills North) and Landranger 165 (Aylesbury & Leighton Buzzard)

alongside a post and wire fence and on a woodland track that shortly bears left. A little way on, it bears right.

Continue to a track junction beside a stile **B** and here go ahead once more, following a

Field edge path, Whiteleaf Hill

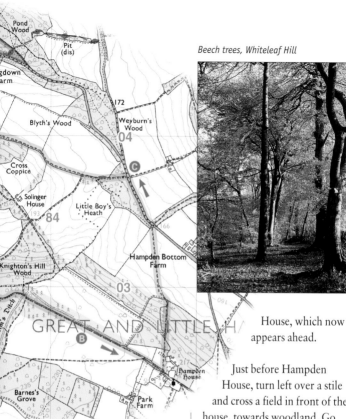

Beech trees, Whiteleaf Hill

woodland path that finally emerges into the corner of a large field.

Follow the field-edge path until it merges with a farm track. Go ahead along this, but as the track bends to the right, leave it by going left through a gate and along a track towards Hampden

House, which now appears ahead.

Just before Hampden House, turn left over a stile and cross a field in front of the house, towards woodland. Go through the woodland on an enclosed path and, on emerging from it, head across a large pasture to the bottom left-hand corner.

Turn left along a road for nearly ¼ mile (400m) to a signposted footpath for Solinger House, on the left, opposite the entrance to

> Not plainly evident, the route follows an ancient earthwork known as **Grim's Ditch**, which is thought to be Saxon in origin, possibly marking a settlement boundary, perhaps Aylesbury.

Hampden Chase Farm **C**. Turn left here, going back into woodland.

As the continuing track makes a pronounced bend to the left, leave it by branching right into a large pasture. Keep to the left through two fields.

D In a field corner, go left and then immediately right through a hedge gap, before swinging left again along a field boundary.

The path later dives left through a hedgerow and across two stiles into the edge of woodland, descending gently to intercept a bridleway at a T-junction.

Hampden House has a Gothic façade concealing a 14th-century building. The house was the home of John Hampden, Member of Parliament for Buckinghamshire, who played an important and perilous role in the Parliamentary opposition to Charles I and his decision to extend Ship Money Tax (levied on ports) to inland estates.

Turn left, along a broad track (the bridleway) and follow it, climbing gently, to rejoin the outward route at a waymark pole. Turn right and go back through the beech woodlands, keeping near the top edge of the woodland. This finally leads out to meet the Ridgeway again. Turn left to return to the car park. ●

Whiteleaf Hill in autumn light

Coombe Hill and Little Hampden

START	Coombe Hill
DISTANCE	5 miles (8km)
TIME	2–3 hours
PARKING	Car park Low Scrubs (start)
ROUTE FEATURES	Mainly woodland trails, often muddy

This walk is especially beautiful, and tranquil, in autumn, when the beeches have turned colour and the woodlands are quiet retreats. But it is a great pleasure to wander here in all seasons, and easy to lose track of time.

Coombe Hill is the highest of the Chiltern Hills and affords a splendid view over the town Aylesbury and as far afield as the Cotswolds, 55 miles (89km) away. The monument on Coombe Hill commemorates the Chilterns men who died fighting in the Boer War. The monument was destroyed by lightning in 1938, but was restored almost immediately.

Leave the car park, towards the road and turn right on to a path into the National Trust Coombe Hill estate. Go forward on to the middle one of three paths, which strikes across open ground, and through a narrow strip of woodland, before bearing right to the monument on Coombe Hill.

Turn around, facing back to the start, but bear slightly right to follow a waymarked route across the top of the west-facing hill slope, part of the Ridgeway National Trail.

The route continues as a broad, green track, bordered on the left by oak, gorse and hawthorn. Gradually, the path is steered left to a kissing-gate on the boundary of National Trust property.

PUBLIC TRANSPORT Buses to Ellesborough
REFRESHMENTS Pub at Little Hampden
PUBLIC TOILETS None on route
ORDNANCE SURVEY MAPS Explorer 181 (Chiltern Hills North) and Landranger 165 (Aylesbury & Leighton Buzzard)

A Turn right, through the gate, still following the Ridgeway and passing through delightful beech woodland on a waymarked route that leads out to a road. Turn right.

About 200 yds (183m) down the road, leave it by turning left at a metal kissing-gate and, a few strides later, go right, over a low stile into woodland. The route continues to be waymarked. In autumn, when the path is obscured by fallen leaves, the waymarks provide a safe guide through the trees, but they are not always easy to spot.

At each of a succession of signposts, keep following the Ridgeway path, ignoring all other turnings.

Not far away in the valley below is the Prime Minister's country retreat, **Chequers**. It is not known how many of our Prime Ministers have wandered in these woodlands, which have been a source of relaxation since Lord Lee gave Chequers to the nation in 1921. The peace of the woodland is invigorating and calming at the same time. In summer, wood sorrel grows in abundance, along with wood anemones and herb robert. Throughout the year the pathways are padded with the leafy downfall built up over the years.

Fungi on a tree on Coombe Hill

Eventually, the Ridgeway path turns on to a descending track. After 200 yds (183m) it meets a cross-track. Here, leaving the Ridgeway, turn left on to a rising track, signposted for the South Bucks Way **B**.

The track, which is muddy, emerges to meet another at a T-junction. Turn left.

A short distance on, at another junction **C**, take the right-hand of four options, passing double metal gates and turning left along a field boundary, now following a section of another long-distance trail, the Icknield Way.

The monument on Coombe Hill

Continue as far as a signpost on the left, where the Icknield Way turns back into woodland. The track through the ensuing woodland comes out to meet a lane. Turn right for the short distance to the Rising Sun pub at Little Hampden, and, directly opposite the pub, turn left on to the continuation of the Icknield Way.

The continuing track once more enters woodland, pursuing an obvious course and waymarked by arrows painted on trees.

The woodland path eventually reaches a large paddock corner **D**. At the corner, turn right, still following the Icknield Way and soon climbing along a chalk and flint path.

When the path forks, branch left **E**. The word 'Riders' painted on a tree shows the correct way to go. This climbs easily to a signpost at the top edge of the woodland.

Turn left at a path junction, still on the Icknield Way, now following the woodland edge. At Hampdenleaf, keep forward on a broad track that leads out to a surfaced lane and chapel in the village of Dunsmore.

At a crossroads, the walk goes forward on to a signposted bridleway, but, between here and the end of the walk, the route-finding through the woodland can be confusing. An easier way of concluding the walk would be to turn left at the crossroads and follow the road back to the start, a distance of about 1 mile (1.6km). Otherwise, keep ahead along the bridleway and, after the last of the houses, continue in the same direction.

When the bridleway forks, branch left along an enclosed path **F**. Continue to reach a cross-track with a large metal gate and cattle-grid on the right. Here, keep ahead, still following the bridleway. A few strides on, ignore a branching bridleway on the left and go forward instead, into woodland.

After about 150 yds (137m), keep an eye open for a path, branching left (yellow arrow waymarks on trees) **G**. Turn left, and, later, at a crosspath, turn right (still waymarked).

About 300 yds (274m) farther on, keep a look-out for a branching path on the left (waymark on the left). Follow the path through the trees. It is indistinct, but is waymarked, and leads back to the car park at the start. ●

? On the route you will find something with 'OS BM 6207' marked on it. What is it?

19 *Stokenchurch and Sprig's Alley*

START Stokenchurch

DISTANCE 5¼ miles (8.4km)

TIME 2–2½ hours

PARKING Car park adjacent King's Arms Hotel

ROUTE FEATURES Woodland, farm tracks and path, uphill sections, roads

The pleasure of this undulating walk comes from a quiet wandering of woodlands, farm fields, peaceful lanes and ancient tracks. The hedgerows are bright in spring and summer with wild flowers and the woodlands alive with birdsong. In winter, keep an eye open for visiting mistle thrushes, fieldfare and brambling.

Begin from the car park adjoining the King's Arms Hotel. Walk left across a green, turning left towards the Royal Oak pub. Turn right into Park Lane and go past modern housing and forward on to a broad track, waymarked as the Chiltern Way.

A waymark

the farm. Walk only as far as a step-stile on the right **A**.

Descend obliquely across a steep field slope to a stile in the bottom corner. Over this, turn left and go down to the bottom of the adjacent field to enter, at a hedge gap, a large arable field.

The track later becomes surfaced. At a track junction, keep right for Hallbottom Farm and, when it next forks, turn left down towards

Follow the path (waymarked) across the field to a stile opposite and then cross the next field towards Crowell Wood.

PUBLIC TRANSPORT Buses to Stokenchurch

REFRESHMENTS Pubs in Stokenchurch, restaurant at Sprig's Alley

PUBLIC TOILETS None on route

ORDNANCE SURVEY MAPS Explorer 171 (Chiltern Hills West) and Landranger 165 (Aylesbury & Leighton Buzzard)

On entering the woodland, go forward, crossing a track **B**, an ancient road used to transport coal to London from South Wales. As you start to climb energetically,

> **?** *Great spotted and green woodpeckers inhabit the Chiltern beechwoods. One of their telltale signs are neat holes in dead trees. See if you can find any.*

the way through the woodland is waymarked.

At the far side of the woodland, cross a stile and go up the next field to an enclosed path, climbing gently. Follow the path to a road and there turn left towards Sprig's Alley .

Continue as far as Pond Farm, on the right, and here leave the road by turning right, through a gate on to a broad track, which later slims down to become a path into beechwood.

A heavily woodpeckered tree in Stokenchurch

Bear left and follow the left-hand woodland edge, finally descending to a gate. Turn right along the edge of Sunley Wood.

Keep following the woodland edge path until, just on reaching a metal gate **D**, the track bears right along a field-edge path flanked by coppiced hazel.

The path eventually meets a surfaced farm lane. Turn right and follow this to a road junction at Town End. Turn right again, into Sprigs Holly Lane, climbing steadily as far as Andridge Farm.

Go left along a signposted path in front of Gate Cottage. A short way on, cross a stile to the right, a driveway and another stile. Then turn left down the field edge to a stile in the bottom corner. Over this, turn left to reach the top of a sloping pasture, with fine views ahead.

Head down a field path, passing a powerline pole, to the bottom corner of the field.

Go left on a farm lane and, as it bends left, leave it by turning right on to a farm track. At a signpost on the right, leave the track by bearing left across an arable field to another farm track.

Cross to steps into a large pasture and keep left along the top edge. Continue into the next field, still keeping to the top of the field.

The sloping pasture is a favoured hunting-ground of **red kites**, as are many of the farm fields north of Stokenchurch. These lovely birds are a delight to watch, and their coloration is seen to best effect when they are bathed in sunlight.

About half-way along the second field, switch sides of the hedgerow, on to a parallel vehicle track, and walk as far as a gate near a bungalow. Bear left across another field, then briefly follow a field edge path to a kissing-gate in a field corner.

Beyond the gate, follow a green path to rejoin the outward route beyond another gate. Turn left to walk back to the Royal Oak and return to the start from there. ●

Colour on a spindle tree

● Canals ● narrowboats ● waterfowl ● kingfishers

20 *Tring Reservoirs and Grand Union Canal*

START Marsworth
DISTANCE 5¾ miles
(9.3km)
TIME 2½–3 hours
PARKING Pay-and-display
car park at Marsworth
entrance
ROUTE FEATURES Towpaths,
farm fields, steps,
reservoir embankment

This delightful tour of the Tring Reservoirs and the Grand Union Canal, although long, generally provides easy walking. The chances of seeing a visiting osprey snatching a meal from the reservoirs, or of spotting some other unusual visitor, tends to delay progress: a pair of binoculars are a useful accessory.

Leave the car park by heading along a track towards both the canal and the reservoirs.

The **Tring Reservoirs** are fed by natural drainage and springs from the surrounding countryside. The four reservoirs Wilstone (1802), Marsworth (1806), Tringford (1816) and Startops End (1817) were built to store water for the Grand Union Canal. Situated on chalk at the foot of the Chilterns, the mineral-rich water of the reservoirs supports a wide diversity of water plants, insects and fish. The reservoirs are a National Nature Reserve and a Site of Special Scientific Interest.

Keep along the towpath as far as Marsworth Top Lock **A** and go over a bridge. Immediately turn left under the bridge to join the Wendover arm of the Grand Union Canal.

When forced to do so, near some factory units in an old mill, cross a canal bridge and rejoin the towpath on the opposite side.

PUBLIC TRANSPORT Buses to Marsworth
REFRESHMENTS Bluebells Tearoom at start
PUBLIC TOILETS None, in tearoom (patrons only)
ORDNANCE SURVEY MAPS xplorer 181 (Chiltern Hills North) and Landranger 165 (Aylesbury & Leighton Buzzard)

B About 100 yds (91m) after the mill, leave the towpath by turning right, down steps on to a footpath alongside a stream. Later, as it borders woodland flanking Tringford Reservoir, the path moves away from the stream and emerges at a gravel track, near the south-west corner of the reservoir.

Turn right, following a fenceline around the edge of the reservoir to reach a bird-watching hide **C**.

The Grand Union Canal at Marsworth

Marsworth Reservoir

Follow the towpath for about ⅓ mile (536m) to the next stile, and there turn right on to a descending path towards Wilstone Reservoir. The path intercepts a vehicle track. Turn right, following it to a field edge, and there turn left to walk along the reservoir embankment.

Continue along the path until it meets concrete slabs across the route, then turn left on to a path crossing a small paddock to a road.

Turn left along the road, and, at a junction a short way on, keep left for Tring. After about 200 yds (183m), turn right at a signpost on to a broad track **D**. When this bends sharply left, leave it by bearing right to a stile giving on to a dry section of the canal.

? *See if you can discover what Mrs Sue Woodward was.*

On the far side of the reservoir, go down steps to the Wilstone Car Park, and turn left along the road, taking great care against approaching traffic as the road makes two sharp bends (without a verge).

At the second bend, leave the road and cross two stiles either side of a plank bridge on the right. Walk diagonally right across the next field to a stile in a field corner. Over this turn left along another vehicle track to a stile beside a metal gate. This gives on to a brief enclosed path.

Beside a gate on the right, cross another stile, which requires raising a barrier. Walk out into the field, but gradually move to the right, to a stile in a far corner (initially out of sight).

Cross the next field. On the other side, near a gate, do not leave the field, but instead keep left along a field boundary beside a stream.

Keep following the stream until, at a sluice gate, the path turns right over a footbridge and stile **E**, passing then through rough ground to emerge on the canal towpath.

Turn right and follow the canal for 1¼ miles (2km), leaving it finally at the White Lion pub. Keep an eye open along this stretch of canal for the darting flight of a kingfisher.

Take care emerging on to the road and crossing towards the Bluebells Tearoom, there turning right for the car park or the tea room. ●

Marsworth Top Lock

Further Information

Walking Safety

Although the reasonably gentle countryside that is the subject of this book offers no real dangers to walkers at any time of the year, it is still advisable to take sensible precautions and follow certain well-tried guidelines.

Always take with you both warm and waterproof clothing and sufficient food and drink. Wear suitable footwear, i.e. strong walking boots or shoes that give a good grip over stony ground, on slippery slopes and in muddy conditions. Try to obtain a local weather forecast and bear it in mind before you start. Do not be afraid to abandon your proposed route and return to your starting point in the event of a sudden and unexpected deterioration in the weather.

All the walks described in this book will be safe to do, given due care and respect, even during the winter. Indeed, a crisp, fine winter day often provides perfect walking conditions, with firm ground underfoot and a clarity unique to this time of the year.

The most difficult hazard likely to be encountered is mud, especially

Bisham church and the Thames

when walking along woodland and field paths, farm tracks and bridleways – the latter in particular can often get churned up by cyclists and horses. In summer, an additional difficulty may be narrow and over-grown paths, particularly along the edges of cultivated fields. Neither should constitute a major problem, provided that the appropriate footwear is worn.

A pollarded beech in Burnham Nature Reserve

Follow the Country Code

- Enjoy the countryside and respect its life and work
- Guard against all risk of fire
- Take your litter home
- Fasten all gates
- Help to keep all water clean
- Keep your dogs under control
- Protect wildlife, plants and trees
- Keep to public paths across farmland
- Take special care on country roads
- Leave livestock, crops and machinery alone
- Make no unnecessary noise
- Use gates and stiles to cross fences, hedges and walls

(The Countryside Agency)

Useful organisations

Council for the Protection of Rural England
Warwick House,
25 Buckingham Palace Road,
London
SW1W 0PP.
Tel. 020 7976 6433;
Fax 020 7976 6373
E-mail: cpre@gn.apc.org

Countryside Agency
John Dower House,
Crescent Place,
Cheltenham
GL50 3RA.
Tel. 01242 521381;
Fax 01242 584270
www.countryside.gov.uk

English Heritage
23 Savile Row, London W1X 1AB.
Tel. 020 7973 3434;
Fax 020 7973 3001
www.english-heritage.org.uk

English Nature
Northminster House, Peterborough,
Cambridgeshire PE1 1UA.
Tel. 01733 455100;
Fax 01733 455103
Website: www.english-nature.org.uk

National Trust
Membership and general enquiries
PO Box 39, Bromley,
Kent BR1 3XL.
Tel. 0181 315 1111

Thames and Chilterns Office:
Hughenden Manor, High Wycombe,
Buckinghamshire HP14 4LA.
Tel. 01494 528051;
Fax 01494 463310

Ordnance Survey
Romsey Road, Maybush,
Southampton SO16 4GU.
Tel. 08456 05 05 05 (Lo-call)
Website: www.ordsvy.gov.uk

Public transport:
Bus Traveline: 0870 608 2 608
Chiltern Railways: 0870 5 165 165
National Rail Enquiries:
08745 48 49 50

Ramblers' Association
2nd Floor, Camelford House,
87-90 Albert Embankment,
London SE1 7TW.
Tel. 020 7339 8585;
Fax 020 7339 8501
www.ramblers.org.uk

Royal Society for the Protection of Birds (RSPB)
The Lodge, Sandy, Beds
SG19 2DL.
Tel. 01767 680551;
Fax 01767 692365
www.rspb.org.uk

Southern Tourist Board
40 Chamberlayne Road, Eastleigh,
Hampshire SO5 5JH.
Tel. 023 8062 5500;
Fax 023 8061 8018

Local tourist information centres:
Aylesbury: 01296 330559
Henley: 01491 578034
High Wycombe: 01494 421892
Maidenhead: 01628 796502
Marlow: 01628 483597
Thame: 01844 212834
Wendover: 01296 696759

Youth Hostels Association
Trevelyan House,
Dimple Road, Matlock,
Derbyshire DE4 3YH
Tel. 01629 592600
Website: www.yha.org.uk